Three Simple Rules

ABINGDON PRESS
NASHVILLE

THREE SIMPLE RULES 24/7

Edited by Josh Tinley
Cover Design by Marcia C'deBaca

 Abingdon Press

ISBN-13: 978-1-426-700330

Manufactured in the United States of America

08 09 10 11 12 13 14 15 16 17—10 9 8 7 6 5 4 3 2 1

CONTENTS

Who Was John Wesley?

John Wesley was born in 1703 in Epworth, England, the fifteenth of nineteen children born to Susanna and Rev. Samuel Wesley, an Anglican (Church of England) minister. He studied and taught at Oxford, where he (along with his brother Charles) started a club devoted to methodically studying Scripture and practicing Christian disciplines such as prayer and service to those in need. Wesley called this group the "holy club"; some of his fellow students, poking fun at the group's methodical habits, called Wesley and his friends "Methodists." The name stuck.

After Oxford, Wesley traveled to the New World, where he served as a missionary among Native Americans in Georgia. He failed as a missionary and returned to England frustrated.

In 1738, while listening to a reading of Martin Luther's "preface to the Epistle to the Romans" at a meeting of Moravians on London's Aldersgate Street, Wesley felt his heart "strangely warmed." He had always known, intellectually, that Christ had taken away his sins and saved him from death. But on Aldersgate Street he felt for the first time the complete assurance that he could "trust in Christ, Christ alone for salvation."

After Aldersgate, Wesley became a very effective preacher and gained quite a following. He organized his followers in small groups, or classes, where they committed to holy living and holding one another accountable. Eventually, these "Methodist societies" spread to the New World; and Wesley appointed bishops to oversee the Methodist movement in America. Wesley never intended for his followers to leave the

Church of England. But not long after the American Revolution, American Methodists formed the Methodist Episcopal Church, an ancestor of the current-day United Methodist Church.

Wesley first wrote his three General Rules as part of his instructions to early Methodist societies in England. Still today The United Methodist Church publishes these "three simple rules" in its *Book of Discipline,* the book of doctrines, rules, and processes that the church publishes every four years.

The Holy Club

Rule 1: Do No Harm
Part 1

It is therefore expected of all who continue therein that they should continue to evidence their desire of salvation by **doing no harm,** by avoiding evil of every kind, especially that which is most generally practiced, such as:

- The taking of the name of God in vain.

- The profaning the day of the Lord, either by doing ordinary work therein or by buying or selling.

> "Spirituous liquors" is another way of saying "alcoholic beverages."

- Drunkenness: buying or selling spirituous liquors, or drinking them, unless in cases of extreme necessity.

- Slaveholding: buying or selling slaves.

> Wesley is saying that Christians shouldn't take one another to court. See Matthew 5:23-26.

- Fighting, quarreling, brawling, brother going to law with brother; returning evil for evil, or railing for railing; the using many words in buying or selling.

> *Railing* is an eighteenth-century word for verbal abuse.

> The more words one uses in buying and selling, the more likely one is to cheat another out of money or merchandise.

- The buying or selling of goods that have not paid the duty. ◄—

A "duty" is a tax placed on certain goods. "Goods that have not paid the duty" are items being sold on the black market.

- The giving or taking things on usury—i.e., unlawful interest. ◄—

See Exodus 22:25 for more on unlawful interest.

- Uncharitable or unprofitable conversation; particularly speaking evil of magistrates or of ministers.

- Doing to others as we would not they should do unto us.

"Magistrates" and "ministers" are local and national political leaders.

- Doing what we know is not for the glory of God, as:

You may recognize this as a version of the Golden Rule, from Matthew 7:12.

–The putting on of gold and costly apparel.

–The taking such diversions as cannot be used in the name of the Lord Jesus.

–The singing those songs, or reading those books, which do not tend to the knowledge or love of God.

–Softness and needless self-indulgence.

–Laying up treasure upon earth.

–Borrowing without a probability of paying; or taking up goods without a probability of paying for them.

"Laying up treasure upon earth" refers to Jesus' teaching in Matthew 6:19-21 and Luke 12:13-21.

From John Wesley's General Rules for Methodist Societies

Do No Harm

In the excerpt from his General Rules on pages 6–7, John Wesley gives several examples of what he means by "do no harm." Look over the examples on pages 6–7. Circle the ones that you think apply to Christians in today's world. Cross out the ones that you think no longer apply to us. If you are unsure of the meaning of one of Wesley's examples, leave it as is.

- Look over the items you have circled. Which of these ways of doing harm are difficult for you to avoid? Why?

- Count the items that you crossed out. For each one you crossed out, come up with an example of doing harm that better applies to Christians today. (For instance, if you crossed out five items, come up with five new examples of doing harm.)

Each of us knows of groups that are locked in conflict, sometimes over profound issues and sometimes over issues that are just plain silly. But the conflict is real, the divisions are deep, and the consequences can often be devastating. If, however, all who are involved can agree to do no harm, the *climate* in which the conflict is going on is immediately changed. How is it changed? Well, if I am to do no harm, I can no longer speak *gossip* about the conflict. I can no longer *speak disparagingly* about those involved in the conflict. I can no longer *manipulate the facts* of the conflict. I can no longer *diminish* those who do not agree with me and must honor each as a child of God. *I will guard my lips, my mind and my heart so that my language will not disparage, injure or wound another child of God. I must do no harm, even while I seek a common good.*

—**Rueben Job**, *Three Simple Rules*, p. 22

Peacemakers

What do the Scriptures below say about doing no harm, especially in our relationships with others?

"You have heard that it was said, 'You shall love your neighbor and hate your enemy.' But I say to you, Love your enemies and pray for those who persecute you, so that you may be children of your Father in heaven.....For if you love those who love you, what reward do you have? Do not even the tax collectors do the same? And if you greet only your brothers and sisters, what more are you doing than others? Do not even the Gentiles do the same? Be perfect, therefore, as your heavenly Father is perfect."

—**Matthew 5:43-48**

Bless those who persecute you; bless and do not curse them....Live in harmony with one another; do not be haughty, but associate with the lowly....Do not repay anyone evil for evil, but take thought for what is noble in the sight of all. If it is possible, so far as it depends on you, live peaceably with all.

—**Romans 12:14, 16-18**

The Peace Rose

Some schools and communities have begun to use something called the Peace Rose to resolve conflicts in a peaceful manner. When two people have a conflict, one of those persons may ask the other to come to the Peace Rose. The rules in these schools and communities say that, if a person is asked to go to the Peace Rose, he or she may not refuse.

When two people come to the Peace Rose, they take turns holding it. Whoever is holding the rose may speak, and the other person must listen without interrupting. When one person has said what he or she has to say, he or she hands the rose to the other person, who then gets a turn to speak. The participants continue passing the rose back and forth, alternately talking and listening, until the conflict is resolved to the satisfaction of both parties.

The Rule in Practice

When we lay aside our weapons and our desire to do harm . . . We discover that we stand on common ground, inhabit a common and precious space, share a common faith, feast at a common table, and have an equal measure of God's unlimited love. When I am determined to do no harm to you, I lose my fear of you; and I am able to see you and hear you more clearly. Disarmed of the possibility to do harm, we find that good and solid place to stand where together we can seek the way forward in faithfulness to God.

—Rueben Job, *Three Simple Rules,* pp. 23–24

Love Feast Scriptures

Read and reflect on the following Scriptures as you celebrate your love feast:

"If your enemies are hungry, feed them; if they are thirsty, give them something to drink."

—Romans 12:20a

When you reap the harvest of your land, you shall not reap to the very edges of your field, or gather the gleanings of your harvest; you shall leave them for the poor and for the alien: I am the LORD your God.

—Leviticus 23:22

When you come together as a church, I hear that there are divisions among you. . . . When you come together, it is not really to eat the Lord's supper. For when the time comes to eat, each of you goes ahead with your own supper, and one goes hungry and another becomes drunk. What! Do you not have homes to eat and drink in? Or do you show contempt for the church of God and humiliate those who have nothing?

—1 Corinthians 11:18b, 21-22c

Weekly Challenge

In the coming week, avoid doing harm. Make a commitment not to say anything negative about any other person. That means no insults and no snide remarks *about* anyone or *to* anyone. It means no jokes at another person's expense and no spreading embarrassing rumors. If you do slip up and say something negative, make a note of it.

Weekly Challenge

Reading Assignment

If you have a copy of Three Simple Rules, *by Rueben Job, take time this week to read the chapter "Do No Harm" (pages 19–32). As you read, reflect on the following questions and jot down notes in a journal or in the space below:*

● What are some ways that people do harm without even thinking about it?

● What is most challenging about obeying this rule to do no harm?

● How would your life be different if you were fully devoted to following this rule? How would our church, our community, and our nation be different if everyone were to take this rule seriously?

Session

Rule 1: Do No Harm
Part 2
Mustard and Yeast

What do the Scriptures below say about what can happen when we are faithful to the rule to do no harm?

[Jesus] also said, "With what can we compare the kingdom of God, or what parable will we use for it? It is like a mustard seed, which, when sown upon the ground, is the smallest of all the seeds on earth; yet when it is sown it grows up and becomes the greatest of all shrubs, and puts forth large branches, so that the birds of the air can make nests in its shade."

—Mark 4:30-32

A little yeast leavens the whole batch of dough.

—Galatians 5:9

See that you are courteous toward all [people]. It matters not, in this respect, whether they are high or low, rich or poor, superior or inferior to you. No, nor even whether good or bad, whether they fear God or not. Indeed the mode of showing your courtesy may vary, as Christian prudence will direct; but the thing itself is due to all.

—**John Wesley**

To do no harm means that I will be on guard so that all my actions and even my silence will not add injury to another of God's children or to any part of God's creation....When I commit myself to this way, I must see each person as a child of God—a recipient of love unearned, unlimited, and undeserved— just like myself. As it is this vision of every other person as the object of God's love and deep awareness that I too live in that loving Presence that can hold me accountable to my commitment to do no harm.

—**Rueben Job,** *Three Simple Rules,* p. 31

Weekly Challenge

Earlier in this study, you read John Wesley's list of harmful behaviors that Christians should avoid. (See pages 4–5.) You also identified some other types of doing harm that are relevant today. Look over all of these harmful behaviors and identify one way of doing harm that you personally struggle with. Why is this kind of behavior hard for you to avoid? Whom are you tempted to harm in this way?

This week, focus on eliminating this one way of doing harm. Whenever you are tempted to harm someone in this way, say a prayer that God will give you the strength to resist temptation. Focus, especially, on not doing harm to your enemies and people who have wronged you. When you feel the urge to lash out at these people, take a deep breath, open your Bible, read Matthew 5:44-48 and Romans 12:14-18, and remember what Scripture teaches us about loving our enemies and those who persecute us. Then say a prayer, asking God for the strength to love without limits.

Weekly Challenge

Session **3**

Rule 2: Do Good
Part 1

It is therefore expected of all who continue therein that they should continue to evidence their desire of salvation by **doing good,** by being in every kind merciful after their power; as they have opportunity, doing good of every possible sort, and, as far as possible, to all men:

- To their bodies, of the ability which God giveth, by giving food to the hungry, by clothing the naked, by visiting or helping them that are sick or in prison.

> This instruction to feed the hungry, clothe the naked, and visit the sick and imprisoned is similar to Jesus' teaching about the judgment of the nations in Matthew 25:34-40.

- To their souls, by instructing, reproving, or exhorting all we have any intercourse with; trampling under foot that enthusiastic doctrine that "we are not to do good unless our hearts be free to it."

> Wesley rejected the idea that "we are not to do good unless our hearts be free to it" because he believed that all people could choose to do good in all situations. In other words, he believed that God had given people free will.

- By doing good, especially to them that are of the household of faith or groaning so to be; employing

  For more on our responsibilities to those in the "household of faith" (other Christians), see 1 Timothy 5:1–6:2.

  them preferably to others; buying one of another, helping each other in business, and so much the more because the world will love its own and them only.

- By all possible diligence and frugality, that the gospel be not blamed.

  Wesley tells Methodists to be diligent and frugal because laziness and greed would reflect poorly on God and the church.

- By running with patience the race which is set before them, denying themselves, and taking up their cross daily; submitting to bear the reproach of Christ, to be as the filth and offscouring of the world; and looking that men should say all manner of evil of them *falsely,* for the Lord's sake.

  "Running with patience the race which is set before them" comes from Hebrews 12:1.

  Offscouring means "that which is disposed of."

  In other words, faithful Christians shouldn't be surprised if they're the subject of nasty lies.

From John Wesley's General Rules for Methodist Societies

Do Good

*As he did for the first rule, "Do no harm," John Wesley gives several
examples of what he means by "Do good." Look over these examples on
pages 16–17. Circle the ones that you think apply to Christians in today's
world. Cross out the ones that you think no longer apply to us. If you are
unsure of the meaning of one of Wesley's examples, leave it as is.*

- Look over the items you have circled. Which of these ways of
  doing good are difficult for you? Why?

- Look over the items you have crossed out. Why, do you think,
  are these ways of doing good no longer relevant?

- If Wesley were writing these rules today, what other examples
  of doing good might he add to the list?

Doing good, like doing no harm, is a proactive way of living. I
do not need to wait until circumstances cry out for aid to relieve
suffering or correct some horrible injustice. I can decide that my
way of living will come down on the side of doing good to all in
every circumstance and in every way I can. I can decide that I
will choose a way of living that nourishes goodness and
strengthens community.

—Rueben Job, *Three Simple Rules,* pp. 37–38

Rule 2: Do Good

For we are what [God] has made us, created in Christ Jesus for good works, which God prepared beforehand to be our way of life.
—Ephesians 2:10

Wash Those Feet!

Washing feet may not strike you as impressive. But we live in a time of shoes, socks, sidewalks, carpeting, automobiles, and indoor plumbing. Jesus, on the other hand, lived in a time of sandals, no socks, dirt roads, dirt floors, lots of walking, and infrequent bathing. The disciples certainly would've had disgusting feet. But Jesus washes them, nonetheless, setting an example of the kind of humble, sacrificial love we should show people.

The Rule in Practice

Weekly Challenge

During this session, you identified ways that you could do good in your everyday life. In the coming week, be on the lookout for ways to do good; and try to identify three ways that you can do good on a daily basis. Here are a few examples:

- Compliment a sibling.
- Take time each day to visit *www.freerice.com,* where, for each vocabulary word you successfully define, the site will donate 20 grains of rice to the United Nations World Food Program.
- Make a commitment not to buy unnecessary or unhealthful snacks. Donate the money you save to a ministry or organization that does good in your community or throughout the world.
- Say, "Thank you," to your teachers after each class.

Weekly Challenge

Reading Assignment

If you have a copy of Three Simple Rules, *by Rueben Job, during the coming week, read the chapter "Do Good" (pages 35–49). Think about the following questions as you read:*

- What is most challenging about obeying this rule to do good? Do you think that doing good is more or less difficult than not doing harm?

- Rueben Job mentions that our "gift of goodness may be rejected, ridiculed, and misused." When have you been rejected or ridiculed for doing good? How did you respond?

- What is the difference between healthy self-denial and unhealthy self-denial (page 45)? How can you practice healthy self-denial?

- How would your life be different if you were fully devoted to following this rule? How would your church, your community, and our nation be different if everyone took this rule seriously?

Session 4

Rule 2: Do Good

Part 2
Of Course, We Should Do Good

Describe in the space provided how you would act in each of the situations below. Be honest.

1. As you are riding your bike on a busy street, you notice a turtle inching its way across the road. What do you do?

2. You have an opportunity to participate in an overseas mission trip, but going on the trip would mean that you would miss seeing your favorite band in concert and celebrating your birthday at home. What do you do?

3. Your church is raising money for communities that were ravaged by a recent natural disaster. The only cash you have on hand is the money your aunt gave you for your birthday. You could donate your birthday money, but you already have big plans for how you would like to spend it. What do you do?

4. You've just earned your driver's license. As you are driving, you notice a younger student from your school on the side of the road with a bicycle that obviously has a flat tire. You assume that he has a cell phone and has called someone, but you aren't sure. What do you do?

Do all the good you can, by all the means you can, in all the places you can, at all the times you can, to all the people you can, as long as ever you can.

—**John Wesley**

• What keeps you from doing "all the good you can, by all the means you can, in all the places you can, at all the times you can, to all the people you can"?

So let us not grow weary in doing what is right, for we will reap at harvest-time, if we do not give up. So then, whenever we have an opportunity, let us work for the good of all, and especially those of the family of faith.

—**Galatians 6:9-10**

• How might doing good things make someone weary? How might doing good actually give us energy and keep us from growing weary?

This way of living [doing good in all circumstances] will require a careful and continual assessment of my life and the world in which I live. It will require an even more bold and radical step than not doing harm to those who may disagree with me and even seek to harm me. For now I am committing myself to seeking good for everyone in my world and everyone in God's world. Even those little offenses, like cutting in ahead of me in traffic, to the large offenses, like considering me less than a child of God, can never move me outside the circle of goodness that flows from God to me and through me to the world. Every act and every word must pass through the love and will of God and there be measured to discover if its purpose does indeed bring good and goodness to all it touches.

—**Rueben Job,** *Three Simple Rules*, p. 38

Weekly Challenge

The above excerpt from *Three Simple Rules* says that we must make a "careful and continual assessment" of our lives to make sure that we are faithfully doing good to all people at all times. In the spirit of careful and continual assessment, this week keep a "Do Good Journal." At the end of each day, make a list of good things that you did and a list of good things you could have done but didn't do. Next to each good thing that you could have done but didn't, write a few words to explain why you passed up this opportunity to do good (such as "too busy" or "didn't know that person"). After you've made your lists, pray for the courage to overcome the obstacles that keep you from doing good.

Session

Rule 3: Stay in Love With God
Part 1

It is expected of all who desire to continue therein that they should continue to evidence their desire of salvation by attending upon all the ordinances of God; such are:

- The public worship of God. ← This, in other words, means "go to church."

- The ministry of the Word, either read or expounded. ← The word *expounded* includes listening to sermons.

- The Supper of the Lord. ← This is also known as Holy Communion or the Eucharist.

- Family and private prayer.

- Searching the Scriptures.

- Fasting or abstinence. ← "Fasting" and "abstinence" are not limited to refraining from food and sexual activity. One could also fast from television or the Internet; one could abstain from insulting others or complaining.

From John Wesley's General Rules for Methodist Societies

Ordinances of God

List some ways in which you and/or your congregation practice each of the "ordinances of God" that John Wesley names. (For example, you might write "Sunday morning worship" under "The public worship of God" or "blessing our meals" under "Family and private prayer.")

The public worship of God | **Family and private prayer**

The ministry of the word, either read or expounded | **Searching the Scriptures**

The Supper of the Lord | **Fasting or abstinence**

Living in the presence of and in harmony with the living God who is made known in Jesus Christ and companions us in the Holy Spirit is to live life from the inside out. It is to find our moral direction, our wisdom, our courage, our strength to live faithfully from the One who authored us, called us, sustains us, and sends us into the world as witnesses who daily practice the way of living with Jesus. Spiritual disciplines keep us in that healing, redeeming presence and power of God that forms and transforms each of us more and more into the image of the One we seek to follow.

—**Rueben Job,** *Three Simple Rules,* p. 55

So those who welcomed [Peter's] message were baptized, and that day about three thousand persons were added [to the church]. They devoted themselves to the apostles' teaching and fellowship, to the breaking of bread and the prayers.

—**Acts 2:41-42**

Without Ceasing?

Rejoice always, pray without ceasing, give thanks in all circumstances; for this is the will of God in Christ Jesus for you. Do not quench the Spirit. Do not despise the words of prophets, but test everything; hold fast to what is good; abstain from every form of evil.

—**1 Thessalonians 5:16-22**

Some Christians, particularly in the Eastern Orthodox tradition, have taken very seriously Paul's command in 1 Thessalonians to "pray without ceasing." To be faithful to this command, many of these believers repeatedly say a prayer known as the Jesus Prayer or the Prayer of the Heart:

> **Lord Jesus Christ, Son of God,**
> **Have mercy on me, a sinner.**

Weekly Challenge

Set aside time each day of this week to pray and to read Scripture, perhaps with the help of a devotional book, magazine, or website. During or after this devotional time, jot down in the space on page 29 a few sentences about what you learned, what you prayed about, what questions you have, or how you will apply what you read and prayed about to your day-to-day life.

If you already spend time each day in prayer and devotion, add to your routine another spiritual practice, such as meditating, gathering your family for prayer, performing a daily act of service, or abstaining from something that you don't need. Write about each day's experience in the space on page 29.

Weekly Challenge

In the space below, write about each day's experience as you complete this week's Weekly Challenge.

DAY 1

DAY 2

DAY 3

DAY 4

DAY 5

DAY 6

DAY 7

Reading Assignment

If you have a copy of Three Simple Rules, *by Rueben Job, during the coming week read the chapter "Stay in Love With God" (pages 53–63). Think about the following questions as you read.*

- What is most challenging about obeying this rule to "stay in love with God" (or as Wesley said, "attend upon all the ordinances of God")?

- How is this rule similar to and different from the first two rules?

- In what ways do you show your love for God?

- What practices could you take on that would bring you closer to God?

- How would being fully devoted to following this rule change your attitude and behavior? How would it help you obey the first two rules?

- How would your church, your community, and our nation be different if everyone were to take this rule seriously?

Session **6**

Rule 3: Stay in Love With God
Part 2

Holy living will not be discovered, achieved, continued, and sustained without staying in love with God. And while staying in love with God involves prayer, worship, study, and the Lord's Supper, it also involves feeding the lambs, tending the sheep, and providing for the needs of others.

—**Rueben Job,** *Three Simple Rules,* p. 58

24/7 Holiness

Read each of the Scriptures below and identify the way(s) of staying in love with God that the Scripture talks about.

Exodus 31:16-17	**Matthew 6:14-15**
Psalm 119:15	**Romans 12:9-17**
Psalm 150	**1 Corinthians 6:19-20**
Matthew 5:23-26	**2 Corinthians 9:6-12**

Going Into the World With Three Simple Rules

In the space below, write one way that you will practice each of the "Three Simple Rules" on an ongoing basis in the coming days, weeks, months, and years. Make sure that these commitments are specific, achievable, and relevant to your life.

1. Do no harm.

2. Do good.

3. Stay in love with God.